by Iain Gray

Lang**Syne**

PUBLISHING

WRITING *to* REMEMBER

LangSyne

PUBLISHING

WRITING *to* REMEMBER

79 Main Street, Newtongrange,
Midlothian EH22 4NA
Tel: 0131 344 0414   Fax: 0845 075 6085
E-mail: info@lang-syne.co.uk
www.langsyneshop.co.uk

Design by Dorothy Meikle
Printed by Ricoh Print Scotland
© Lang Syne Publishers Ltd 2015

ISBN 978-1-85217-328-9

McManus

MOTTO:
With heart and hand
(and) Faithful even until death
(and) By virtue and honour.

CREST:
A hand holding a cross
(and) A demi lion holding a sceptre in its paw.

NAME variations include:
Mac Maghnuis (*Gaelic*)
Mac Manus (*Gaelic*)
MacManners
Manus
McManus

Chapter one:

Origins of Irish surnames

**According to an old saying, there are two types of Irish –
those who actually are Irish and those who wish they were.**

This sentiment is only one example of the allure that the
high romance and drama of the proud nation's history holds
for thousands of people scattered across the world today.

It's a sad fact, however, that the vast majority of Irish
surnames are found far beyond Irish shores, rather than on
the Emerald Isle itself.

The population stood at around eight million souls in
1841, but today it stands at fewer than six million.

This is mainly a tragic consequence of the potato
famine, also known as the Great Hunger, which devastated
Ireland between 1845 and 1849.

The Irish peasantry had become almost wholly reliant
for basic sustenance on the potato, first introduced from the
Americas in the seventeenth century.

When the crop was hit by a blight, at least 800,000
people starved to death while an estimated two million
others were forced to seek a new life far from their native
shores – particularly in America, Canada, and Australia.

The effects of the potato blight continued until about
1851, by which time a firm pattern of emigration had
become established.

Ireland's loss, however, was to the gain of the countries in which the immigrants settled, contributing enormously, as their descendants do today, to the well being of the nations in which their forefathers settled.

But those who were forced through dire circumstance to establish a new life in foreign parts never forgot their roots, or the proud heritage and traditions of the land that gave them birth.

Nor do their descendants.

It is a heritage that is inextricably bound up in the colourful variety of Irish names themselves – and the origin and history of these names forms an integral part of the vibrant drama that is the nation's history, one of both glorious fortune and tragic misfortune.

This history is well documented, and one of the most important and fascinating of the earliest sources are *The Annals of the Four Masters*, compiled between 1632 and 1636 by four friars at the Franciscan Monastery in County Donegal.

Compiled from earlier sources, and purporting to go back to the Biblical Deluge, much of the material takes in the mythological origins and history of Ireland and the Irish.

This includes tales of successive waves of invaders and settlers such as the Fomorians, the Partholonians, the Nemedians, the Fir Bolgs, the Tuatha De Danann, and the Laigain.

Of particular interest are the *Milesian Genealogies*,

because the majority of Irish clans today claim a descent from either Heremon, Ir, or Heber – three of the sons of Milesius, a king of what is now modern day Spain.

These sons invaded Ireland in the second millennium B.C, apparently in fulfilment of a mysterious prophecy received by their father.

This Milesian lineage is said to have ruled Ireland for nearly 3,000 years, until the island came under the sway of England's King Henry II in 1171 following what is known as the Cambro-Norman invasion.

This is an important date not only in Irish history in general, but for the effect the invasion subsequently had for Irish surnames.

'Cambro' comes from the Welsh, and 'Cambro-Norman' describes those Welsh knights of Norman origin who invaded Ireland.

But they were invaders who stayed, inter-marrying with the native Irish population and founding their own proud dynasties that bore Cambro-Norman names such as Archer, Barbour, Brannagh, Fitzgerald, Fitzgibbon, Fleming, Joyce, Plunkett, and Walsh – to name only a few.

These 'Cambro-Norman' surnames that still flourish throughout the world today form one of the three main categories in which Irish names can be placed – those of Gaelic-Irish, Cambro-Norman, and Anglo-Irish.

Previous to the Cambro-Norman invasion of the twelfth century, and throughout the earlier invasions and settlement of those wild bands of sea rovers known as the Vikings in the eighth and ninth centuries, the population of the island was relatively small, and it was normal for a person to be identified through the use of only a forename.

But as population gradually increased and there were many more people with the same forename, surnames were adopted to distinguish one person, or one community, from another.

Individuals identified themselves with their own particular tribe, or 'tuath', and this tribe – that also became known as a clann, or clan – took its name from some distinguished ancestor who had founded the clan.

The Gaelic-Irish form of the name Kelly, for example, is Ó Ceallaigh, or O'Kelly, indicating descent from an original 'Ceallaigh', with the 'O' denoting 'grandson of.' The name was later anglicised to Kelly.

The prefix 'Mac' or 'Mc', meanwhile, as with the clans of the Scottish Highlands, denotes 'son of.'

Although the Irish clans had much in common with their Scottish counterparts, one important difference lies in what are known as 'septs', or branches, of the clan.

Septs of Scottish clans were groups who often bore an entirely different name from the clan name but were under the clan's protection.

In Ireland, septs were groups that shared the same name and who could be found scattered throughout the four provinces of Ulster, Leinster, Munster, and Connacht.

The 'golden age' of the Gaelic-Irish clans, infused as their veins were with the blood of Celts, pre-dates the Viking invasions of the eighth and ninth centuries and the Norman invasion of the twelfth century, and the sacred heart of the country was the Hill of Tara, near the River Boyne, in County Meath.

Known in Gaelic as 'Teamhar na Rí', or Hill of Kings, it was the royal seat of the 'Ard Rí Éireann', or High King of Ireland, to whom the petty kings, or chieftains, from the island's provinces were ultimately subordinate.

It was on the Hill of Tara, beside a stone pillar known as the Irish 'Lia Fáil', or Stone of Destiny, that the High Kings were inaugurated and, according to legend, this stone would emit a piercing screech that could be heard all over Ireland when touched by the hand of the rightful king.

The Hill of Tara is today one of the island's main tourist attractions.

Opposition to English rule over Ireland, established in the wake of the Cambro-Norman invasion, broke out frequently and the harsh solution adopted by the powerful forces of the Crown was to forcibly evict the native Irish from their lands.

These lands were then granted to Protestant colonists, or 'planters', from Britain.

Many of these colonists, ironically, came from Scotland and were the descendants of the original 'Scotti', or 'Scots', who gave their name to Scotland after migrating there in the fifth century A.D., from the north of Ireland.

Colonisation entailed harsh penal laws being imposed on the majority of the native Irish population, stripping them practically of all of their rights.

The Crown's main bastion in Ireland was Dublin and its environs, known as the Pale, and it was the dispossessed peasantry who lived outside this Pale, desperately striving to eke out a meagre living.

It was this that gave rise to the modern-day expression of someone or something being 'beyond the pale'.

Attempts were made to stamp out all aspects of the ancient Gaelic-Irish culture, to the extent that even to bear a Gaelic-Irish name was to invite discrimination.

This is why many Gaelic-Irish names were anglicised with, for example, and noted above, Ó Ceallaigh, or O'Kelly, being anglicised to Kelly.

Succeeding centuries have seen strong revivals of Gaelic-Irish consciousness, however, and this has led to many families reverting back to the original form of their name, while the language itself is frequently found on the fluent tongues of an estimated 90,000 to 145,000 of the island's population.

Ireland's turbulent history of religious and political strife is one that lasted well into the twentieth century, a landmark century that saw the partition of the island into the twenty-six counties of the independent Republic of

Ireland, or Eire, and the six counties of Northern Ireland, or Ulster.

Dublin, originally founded by Vikings, is now a vibrant and truly cosmopolitan city while the proud city of Belfast is one of the jewels in the crown of Ulster.

It was Saint Patrick who first brought the light of Christianity to Ireland in the fifth century A.D.

Interpretations of this Christian message have varied over the centuries, often leading to bitter sectarian conflict – but the many intricately sculpted Celtic Crosses found all over the island are symbolic of a unity that crosses the sectarian divide.

It is an image that fuses the 'old gods' of the Celts with Christianity.

All the signs from the early years of this new millennium indicate that sectarian strife may soon become a thing of the past – with the Irish and their many kinsfolk across the world, be they Protestant or Catholic, finding common purpose in the rich tapestry of their shared heritage.

Chapter two:

Ancient heritage

Although there are at least two possible sources for the origin of the MacManus, or McManus, name and although both these sources lie far beyond the Emerald Isle itself, bearers of the name today are nevertheless descendants of a truly native Irish clan.

The Gaelic-Irish forms of the name are Mac Maghnuis and Mac Manus, indicating descent from 'Manus'.

'Manus', or 'Magnus', signifies 'great' and may possibly refer to either Charles the Great, better known as the ninth century Holy Roman Emperor Charlemagne or the tenth century King Magnus of Norway.

It was through their fame that the name of 'Manus' or 'Magnus' became popular far beyond the boundaries of their own respective territories, and it is therefore no surprise that powerful Irish chieftains may have adopted the name in a bid for reflected glory.

This appears to have been the case with what became the McManuses/MacManuses – two separate septs of whom were to be found in the ancient western province of Connacht and the northern province of Ulster.

But intermarriage between the septs means that bearers of the name today, whether their origins are Connacht or Ulster, share the same rich heritage and traditions.

This is a heritage closely bound to the vibrant drama that is Ireland's history.

The two septs were those of McManus-Maguire and McManus-O'Connor, with the McManus-Maguire flourishing for centuries in Ulster and the McManus-O'Connor flourishing in Connacht.

With strong bonds to the powerful Maguires and the Royal House of O'Connor, the McManuses were destined to share in both their glorious fortunes and tragic misfortunes.

The McManus-Maguires take their name from Manus Maguire, a late thirteenth and early fourteenth century Ulster king.

A son of the Maguire chieftain Don Mór Maguire, he was born in Lisnaskea, in what is now the Northern Irish county of Fermanagh.

The first mention of the Maguires in the historical annals of Ireland goes back to about the middle of the tenth century, and the clan is thought to have first arrived in Ulster from the present day county of Westmeath, in the province of Leinster.

This means that in all probability they had formed part of the mighty invasion force from the south that wrested control of Ulster from the rival tribal grouping known as the Ulaid.

This laid the foundations of the Ulster kingdom known as Airghialla, or Oirghialla, anglicised as Oriel.

So great was the Maguire hold on Fermanagh from the

thirteenth to the seventeenth centuries that the county was actually known as Maguire's Country.

Separate septs, or branches, of the Maguires were scattered throughout Fermanagh, but it was the imposing summit of Cuilcagh, on the borders of Fermanagh and Co. Cavan, that was the site of the solemn inauguration ceremonies of the Maguire chieftains, in addition to a site known as Sciath Gabhra, near Lisknaskea.

Manus Maguire and what became the sept of McManus in Ulster came to be established at Knockninny, on the southern shore of the beautiful Upper Lough Erne, and it was from here that they held sway as a proud clan in their own right.

In Connacht, the McManuses traced a descent from Connor, a late tenth century king of the province.

One of his descendants was the famed Turlough Mór O'Connor, the 48th king of Connacht and also Ard Rí of the island in the mid twelfth century.

One of his sons was Manus O'Connor, lord of what was known as Tír Tuathail and which now forms the parish of Kilronan in the northern reaches of modern day Co. Roscommon.

It was his sons who adopted the surname McManus, signifying 'son of Manus'.

Along with other clans that include the O'Connors, O'Flanagans and McDermotts, the McManuses are also an offshoot of what was the powerful confederation of clans known as the Uí Neill – who trace a descent from the great late fourth century warrior king Niall of the Nine Hostages.

The sub-branch of the Uí Neill to which the McManuses belonged was known as the Síol Muireadhaigh, with the O'Connors being the most dominant clan.

In addition to their dominance as sub-kings of Connacht, they not only acted for a time as the Ard Rí of Ireland as a whole, but also in effect represented the last of the ancient institution.

One of the most celebrated of these Ard Rí was the McManus ancestor Turlough Mór O'Connor, who boasted no less than twenty children through three marriages, in addition to the building of a number of bridges and castles throughout his vast domains.

It was one of his many sons, Rory O'Connor, who was destined to play a formative and ultimately tragic role in one of the most important episodes in his nation's history after taking over the mantle of the High Kingship following his father's death in 1156.

This was an episode in which the McManuses, because of their bond with the O'Connors, would become fatally embroiled.

Twelfth century Ireland was far from being a unified nation, split up as it was into territories ruled over by squabbling chieftains who ruled as kings in their own right – and this inter-clan rivalry worked to the advantage of the invaders.

In a series of bloody conflicts one chieftain, or king, would occasionally gain the upper hand over his rivals, and by 1156 the most powerful was Muirchertach MacLochlainn, king of the O'Neills.

He was opposed by the equally powerful Rory O'Connor, but increased his power and influence by allying himself with Dermot MacMurrough, King of Leinster.

MacLochlainn and MacMurrough were aware that the main key to the kingdom of Ireland was the thriving trading port of Dublin that had been established by invading Vikings, or Ostmen, in 852 A.D.

Their combined forces took Dublin, but when MacLochlainn died the Dubliners rose up in revolt and overthrew the unpopular MacMurrough.

A triumphant Rory O'Connor, and his allies that included the McManuses, now entered Dublin and he was later inaugurated as Ard Rí – but MacMurrough refused to accept defeat.

He appealed for help from England's Henry II in unseating O'Connor, an act that was to radically affect the future course of not only the fortunes of the McManuses but their fellow Gaelic-Irish as a whole.

Chapter three:

Invasion and rebellion

Henry II agreed to help MacMurrough, but distanced himself from direct action by delegating his Norman subjects in Wales with the task.

These ambitious and battle-hardened barons and knights had first settled in Wales following the Norman Conquest of England in 1066 and, with an eye on rich booty, plunder and lands, were only too eager to obey their sovereign's wishes and furnish MacMurrough with aid.

MacMurrough crossed the Irish Sea to Bristol, where he rallied barons such as Robert Fitzstephen and Maurice Fitzgerald to his cause, along with Gilbert de Clare, Earl of Pembroke.

As an inducement to de Clare, MacMurrough offered him the hand of his beautiful young daughter, Aife, in marriage, with the further sweetener to the deal that he would take over the province of Leinster on MacMurrough's death.

The mighty Norman war machine soon moved into action, and so fierce and disciplined was their onslaught on the forces of Rory O'Connor and his allies that by 1171 they had re-captured Dublin, in the name of MacMurrough, and other strategically important territories.

Henry II now began to take cold feet over the venture,

realising that he may have created a rival in the form of a separate Norman kingdom in Ireland.

Accordingly, he landed on the island, near Waterford, at the head of a large army with the aim of curbing the power of his Cambro-Norman barons.

But protracted war was averted when they submitted to the royal will, promising homage and allegiance in return for holding the territories they had conquered in the king's name.

Henry also received the submission and homage of many of the Irish chieftains, tired as they were with internecine warfare and also perhaps realising that as long as they were rivals and not united they were no match for the powerful forces the English Crown could muster.

English dominion over Ireland was ratified through the Treaty of Windsor of 1175, under the terms of which Rory O'Connor, for example, was only allowed to rule territory unoccupied by the Normans in the role of a vassal of the king.

This humiliation appears to have been too much for the proud O'Connor to bear, for he abdicated his kingship and took himself off to monastic seclusion.

He died in 1198, the last in a line of no less than eleven O'Connor High Kings of Ireland.

The island in effect became a fiefdom of the English Crown, as further waves of ambitious Anglo-Normans descended on it, wresting land from the native Irish.

It was a blueprint for frequent bloody rebellion, and *The Annals of the Four Masters* contain several entries indicating how the McManuses, for example, were to be found among the ranks of the rebels.

One entry for 1249 states how a Brian An Doire MacManus, son of Manus O'Connor, was 'killed fighting against the English.'

Rebellion became endemic throughout the island and, in a bid to quash it, the authorities attempted to eradicate the ancient Gaelic-Irish institution known as Brehon Law – most notably and brutally in the McManus homeland of Connacht.

'Brehon' was the name for Ireland's earliest hereditary lawmakers and judges, stemming from the Gaelic-Irish *breitheamh*, meaning a judge, and the brehons were responsible for interpreting and dispensing justice based on a series of statutes that governed every aspect of daily life.

Also known as the *Fenachas*, or *Law of the Feni*, or Freemen of Ireland, these laws were first written down during what is known as the Old Irish period of 600 to 900 A.D.

The laws show that Ireland was very far from being the backward and uncivilised nation so often depicted by its detractors.

Under the law known as *Cáin Adomnáin*, for example, first drawn up in 697 A.D., Irish women enjoyed a better status than that accorded any other women in Europe, with the right to seek divorce from abusive husbands and the right to hold their own property.

The attempt to bring the native Irish into line with English custom and practice by eradicating institutions such as Brehon Law had terrible consequences.

Under Sir Richard Bingham, for example, who was appointed Governor of Connacht in 1584, innocent men, women and children were hanged at will in a campaign of terror.

One of its many victims was Turlough Oge MacManus who, sentenced to be hanged, was granted a pardon at the last moment by the Crown authorities in Dublin. But this was simply ignored and MacManus duly hanged.

Discontent had grown on the island over the policy known as 'plantation', or settlement of loyal Protestants on lands previously held by the native Irish.

This policy had started during the reign from 1491 to 1547 of Henry VIII, whose Reformation effectively outlawed the established Roman Catholic faith throughout his dominions.

The policy continued throughout the subsequent reigns of Elizabeth I, James I, Charles I, and in the aftermath of the murderous Cromwellian invasion of the island in 1649 – one that led to even further harsh conditions being imposed on the Gaelic-Irish such as the McManuses.

An edict was issued stating that any native Irish found east of the River Shannon after May 1, 1654, faced either summary execution or transportation to the West Indies.

The final death knell of the ancient Gaelic order of clans such as the McManuses was sounded in 1688 in what is known as Cogadh an Dá Rí, or the War of the Two Kings.

Also known as the Williamite War in Ireland, it was sparked off when the Stuart monarch James II, under threat from powerful factions who feared a return to the dominance of Roman Catholicism under his rule, fled into French exile.

The Protestant William of Orange and his wife Mary were invited to take up the thrones of Scotland, Ireland and England – but James had significant Catholic support in Ireland.

His supporters were known as Jacobites, and among them were the McManuses of both Connacht and Ulster.

Following the arrival in England of William and Mary from Holland, Richard Talbot, 1st Earl of Tyrconnell and James's Lord Deputy in Ireland, assembled an army loyal to the Stuart cause, and McManus names can be found on the muster roll for this army.

The aim was to garrison and fortify the island in the name of James and quell any resistance.

Londonderry, or Derry, proved loyal to the cause of William of Orange, or William III as he had become, and managed to hold out against a siege that was not lifted until July 28, 1689, the starving citizens having been reduced to eating rats.

James, with the support of 10,000 troops, supplies and money supplied by Louis XIV of France, had sailed from Brest and landed at Kinsale in March of 1689 and joined forces with his Irish supporters.

Marching to Dublin and gathering more Jacobite support along the way, he set up a Parliament in the city.

William, meanwhile, despatched the veteran Dutch soldier Marshall Schomburg to Ireland with a 10,000-strong force that landed in Belfast Lough and occupied Carrickfergus.

The next few months continued in a state of stalemate, with William's forces in the north and the bulk of the Jacobites in the south. Seeking to break the deadlock, William himself descended on the island in June of 1690 with an additional 35,000 troops and set off for Dublin.

The Jacobites marched north to meet him and the two forces finally clashed on the morning of July 12, 1690, in the battle of the Boyne – William narrowly escaping death before the battle proper began when a sniper's bullet grazed his shoulder while he was breakfasting on the north bank of the Boyne river.

The Jacobites were routed, and McManuses were among their many dead.

James fled again into French exile, never to return, while another significant Jacobite defeat occurred in July of 1691 at the battle of Aughrim – with about half their army killed on the field, wounded, or taken prisoner.

The Williamite forces besieged Limerick and the Jacobites were forced to surrender in September of 1691.

A peace treaty known as the Treaty of Limerick followed, under which those willing to swear an oath of loyalty to William were allowed to remain in their native land.

Those reluctant to do so, including many native Irish such as the McManuses, chose foreign exile – their ancient homelands lost to them forever.

Chapter four:

On the world stage

From music and sport to acting and politics, bearers of the McManus and MacManus names have achieved international honours and fame.

Born in 1954 in London, Declan Patrick MacManus is the singer, songwriter and musician better known as **Elvis Costello** and whose many hit singles include the 1979 *Oliver's Army*. In addition to a successful solo career where he has covered musical genres that include punk rock, new wave and rock, he has also collaborated with other talented composers and artistes who include Burt Bacharach, Emmylou Harris, Roy Orbison, Bob Dylan and Paul McCartney.

His father is the musician and trumpet player **Ross MacManus**, born in 1927 in Birkenhead, England, and who played for a time with the Joe Loss Orchestra. He has also released an album where he covers Elvis Presley songs – with the tongue in cheek title of *Elvis' Dad Sings Elvis*.

Born in 1980 in Glasgow, **Michelle McManus** is the Scottish singer, songwriter, television personality and radio presenter who came to fame in 2003 when she won the second series of the British *Pop Idol* competition, with her debut single *All This Time* becoming a No.1 hit.

In a different musical genre **Tony McManus**, born in

1965 in Paisley, is the accomplished Scottish acoustic Celtic folk guitarist whose albums include the 1998 *Pourquoi Quebec?* which was recorded in Quebec, and the 2002 *Ceol More*.

Bearers of the name have also excelled, and continue to excel, in the highly competitive world of sport.

Born in 1951 in Limerick, John Patrick McManus is the Irish businessman and racehorse owner better known as **J.P. McManus**.

Owner of a stud farm in the Republic of Ireland's Co. Kildare, at the time of writing he is National Hunt racing's largest owner.

From horseracing to gymnastics, **Heather Ross-McManus** is the former Canadian trampoline gymnast who was born in 1973 in Etobicoke, Ontario.

She retired from international competition in 1993, but returned five years later when trampolining became accepted as a sport in the Olympic Games.

Winning a bronze medal in the team event at the 2003 World Championships, she finished in sixth place at the Olympics a year later.

In baseball **Francis E. McManus** was the professional catcher who played from 1899 to 1904 in teams that included the Washington Senators, Detroit Tigers and New York Highlanders. Born in 1875 in Lawrence, Massachusetts, he died in 1923.

Also in baseball **Marty McManus**, born in 1900 in

Chicago, was the Major League infielder who played for the Detroit Tigers from 1927 to 1931 and the Boston Red Sox and Boston Braves from 1931 to 1934. He died in 1966.

In the swimming pool **Diana MacManus**, born in 1986 in San Diego, California, is the American backstroke swimmer who won a gold medal in the women's 100-metres backstroke at the 2002 World Cup and two gold medals in the 100-metres and the 4x100 medley relay events at the 2003 Pan American games.

On the fields of European football **Stephen McManus** is the Scottish international footballer who, at the time of writing, is captain of Celtic Football Club in the Scottish Premier League. The talented defender, born in 1982 in Lanark, is a product of the club's youth academy.

Another talented Scottish player is **Allan McManus**, the defender who was born in 1974 in Paisley and who has played for teams that include Hearts, St. Johnstone, Airdrie and Greenock Morton.

In American football, **Danny McManus** is the retired American footballer and Canadian football quarterback who was born in 1965 in Florida.

Teams he played for include the Winnipeg Blue Bombers, British Columbia Lions, Edmonton Eskimos and Calgary Stampeders.

In the wrestling ring **Mick McManus** is the former English professional wrestler who was born in 1928 in New Cross, London. Nicknamed 'The Man You Love to Hate',

McManus, who often appeared on a popular British television wrestling show, was the holder on two occasions of the British Welterweight Championship and also held the British Middleweight Championship and the European Middleweight Championship.

In the rather more sedate sport of snooker, **Alan McManus** is the Scottish professional player who was born in 1971. Nicknamed 'Angles' McManus for his tactical play and safety shots, he was ranked among the world Top 16 players from 1990 to 2006, and claimed the Masters title at Wembley, London, in 1994.

In ice hockey, **Sammy McManus**, born in 1911 in Belfast and later immigrating to America, was the professional player who played in the National Hockey League for the Boston Bruins and Montreal Maroons.

He died in 1976.

In Australian Rules football, **Shaun McManus**, born in 1976, is the former professional player who played for Fremantle Football Club in the Australian Football League.

He is a cousin of John McManus, the multi award winning Australian media personality better known as **Rove McManus**. Born in Perth in 1974 and host of the variety show *Rove*, his many awards include a number of Australian Logie Awards for Most Popular TV Presenter and for Most Popular Light Entertainment Programme.

Also on the stage, **Mark McManus**, born in 1935 in Hamilton, South Lanarkshire, was the Scottish actor who became famous for his role as Chief Inspector Jim Taggart in the highly popular and long-running Scottish Television series *Taggart*. But before he obtained his starring role in the gritty police drama in 1983, McManus had worked for a time as an actor in Australia – performing in amateur theatre groups before obtaining roles in Australian television series such as *Skippy, the Bush Kangaroo*.

He died in 1994 and became the first person to be posthumously awarded the Lord Provost of Glasgow Award for Performing Arts – with Glasgow being the city in which *Taggart* is set. One common misunderstanding is that Mark McManus was a brother of Brian Connolly, the lead singer with the former British pop group Sweet. The truth of the matter is that one of McManus's uncles was Connolly's stepfather, making the actor and the singer half cousins.

In the creative world of the written word **Patrick F. McManus**, born in Idaho in 1933, is the humourist writer of American outdoors life whose many works include the 1978 *A Fine and Pleasant Misery*, the 1983 *Never Sniff a Gift Fish* and the 2002 *Bear in the Attic*.

In the equally creative world of art, **George McManus**, born in 1884 in St. Louis, Missouri and who died in 1954, was the American cartoonist best remembered as the creator of the *Maggie and Jiggs* characters in the widely syndicated comic strip *Bringing up Father*. The strip was included in the 'Comic Strip Classics' series of commemorative United States postage stamps issued in 1995.

In contemporary times, **Shawn McManus**, born in 1958 in Brookline, Massachusetts is the American artist famed for his work for Heavy Metal and DC Comics.

Back in Ireland, **Henry MacManus**, born in 1810 in Co. Monaghan and who died in 1878, was the renowned Irish artist whose paintings of historical scenes and of everyday Irish life were exhibited in his lifetime at both the Royal Hibernian Academy in Dublin and the Royal Academy in London.

On the field of battle, **Peter McManus** was the Irish recipient of the Victoria Cross – the highest award for gallantry for British and Commonwealth forces – who was born in 1829 in Tynan, Co. Armagh.

He had been a private in the 1st Battalion, 5th Regiment of Foot, during the Indian Mutiny when, in September of 1857 at Lucknow, he helped a party of fellow soldiers who had been besieged in a house by the enemy.

Under heavy fire, and along with a comrade, he also managed to rescue a wounded officer.

Later promoted to sergeant, he was killed in action at Allahabad less than two years later.

In the world of science, **Dr. Joseph McManus**, born in 1911 in Blackville, New Brunswick and who died in 1980, was the leading Canadian pathologist responsible for devising special scientific techniques for use in pathology.

Executive director from 1965 to 1970 of the Federation of American Societies for Experimental Biology in

Bethesda, Maryland, he was also an ardent supporter of civil rights.

In the world of politics, **Liz McManus** is the Republic of Ireland Labour Party politician who was born in 1947 in Montreal, Canada.

Now firmly settled in Ireland, at the time of writing she represents Wicklow in Dáil Éireann, the Irish Parliament.

In Australian politics, **Francis McManus**, born in 1905 in North Melbourne and who died in 1983, was the leading figure who helped to establish what later became the country's Democratic Labor Party, while back in Ireland and in contemporary times, **Frank McManus** is a Northern Irish nationalist politician.

Born in 1942 in Lisnaskea, Co. Fermanagh, he served for a time in the British House of Commons.

Instrumental in the formation in 1920 of the Communist Party of Great Britain (C.P.G.B.), **Arthur MacManus** was the Scottish trade unionist and socialist politician who was born in 1889.

A leading member of the Clyde Workers Committee during the era in Glasgow known as 'Red Clydeside', he was imprisoned for a time along with twelve other C.P.G.B. officials for seditious libel and incitement to mutiny.

Rather fittingly for this dedicated communist, his ashes were placed within the Kremlin Wall in Moscow following his death in 1927.

Key dates in Ireland's history from the first settlers to the formation of the Irish Republic:

circa 7000 B.C.	Arrival and settlement of Stone Age people.
circa 3000 B.C.	Arrival of settlers of New Stone Age period.
circa 600 B.C.	First arrival of the Celts.
200 A.D.	Establishment of Hill of Tara, Co. Meath, as seat of the High Kings.
circa 432 A.D.	Christian mission of St. Patrick.
800-920 A.D.	Invasion and subsequent settlement of Vikings.
1002 A.D.	Brian Boru recognised as High King.
1014	Brian Boru killed at battle of Clontarf.
1169-1170	Cambro-Norman invasion of the island.
1171	Henry II claims Ireland for the English Crown.
1366	Statutes of Kilkenny ban marriage between native Irish and English.
1529-1536	England's Henry VIII embarks on religious Reformation.
1536	Earl of Kildare rebels against the Crown.
1541	Henry VIII declared King of Ireland.
1558	Accession to English throne of Elizabeth I.
1565	Battle of Affane.
1569-1573	First Desmond Rebellion.
1579-1583	Second Desmond Rebellion.
1594-1603	Nine Years War.
1606	Plantation' of Scottish and English settlers.
1607	Flight of the Earls.
1632-1636	Annals of the Four Masters compiled.
1641	Rebellion over policy of plantation and other grievances.
1649	Beginning of Cromwellian conquest.
1688	Flight into exile in France of Catholic Stuart monarch James II as Protestant Prince William of Orange invited to take throne of England along with his wife, Mary.
1689	William and Mary enthroned as joint monarchs; siege of Derry.
1690	Jacobite forces of James defeated by William at battle of the Boyne (July) and Dublin taken.

1691	Athlone taken by William; Jacobite defeats follow at Aughrim, Galway, and Limerick; conflict ends with Treaty of Limerick (October) and Irish officers allowed to leave for France.
1695	Penal laws introduced to restrict rights of Catholics; banishment of Catholic clergy.
1704	Laws introduced constricting rights of Catholics in landholding and public office.
1728	Franchise removed from Catholics.
1791	Foundation of United Irishmen republican movement.
1796	French invasion force lands in Bantry Bay.
1798	Defeat of Rising in Wexford and death of United Irishmen leaders Wolfe Tone and Lord Edward Fitzgerald.
1800	Act of Union between England and Ireland.
1803	Dublin Rising under Robert Emmet.
1829	Catholics allowed to sit in Parliament.
1845-1849	The Great Hunger: thousands starve to death as potato crop fails and thousands more emigrate.
1856	Phoenix Society founded.
1858	Irish Republican Brotherhood established.
1873	Foundation of Home Rule League.
1893	Foundation of Gaelic League.
1904	Foundation of Irish Reform Association.
1913	Dublin strikes and lockout.
1916	Easter Rising in Dublin and proclamation of an Irish Republic.
1917	Irish Parliament formed after Sinn Fein election victory.
1919-1921	War between Irish Republican Army and British Army.
1922	Irish Free State founded, while six northern counties remain part of United Kingdom as Northern Ireland, or Ulster; civil war up until 1923 between rival republican groups.
1949	Foundation of Irish Republic after all remaining constitutional links with Britain are severed.